HILTON HEAD ISLAND

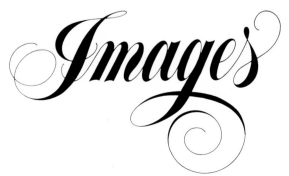

Hilton Head Island first came to my attention in a letter from my father. I was living in a noisy, crowded little village on the outskirts of Seoul, Korea. The name fairly jumped off the page for the simple reason it had the word Island in it. In the letter my father told me that he and mother had made the decision to leave the severe cold winters of Wisconsin behind and move to an island off the coast of South Carolina - it was called Hilton Head Island. Visions of tropical splendor rushed to my head but, South Carolina? No one ever goes to South Carolina to stay. To me it was a place on the way to Florida. I learned that this was not so; indeed, a great many people went to South Carolina and lived there most happily. And I was to learn that after the construction of a bridge from the mainland to the Island a number of them chose Hilton Head Island, as they do now, in ever increasing numbers. I was also to learn Hilton Head was a place steeped in history and lore, just the sort of place my father would delight in. There was exploring to do and new places to see and there were deep, gentle southern nights with the music of the rolling waves to keep time by.

Upon moving to the Island, my parents found a most open and loving community of new friends. They had felt many apprehensions about leaving the old town, my father's and my birthplace, and moving to a new community where they knew virtually no one. They soon found Hilton Head had many people equally anxious to make new friends and to get on with the business of building the Island into a community of substance and merit. They rapidly met people who had moved here from all parts of the country, people glad to know them and delighted with their new home. Cocktail parties regulated strictly by the clock from 6 to 8 pm, on the "embassy schedule" became a primary meeting place. Everyone was anxious to share his or her newest Island discovery: a place for shells,

a new meadow with tabby ruins, a great fishing spot, the newest hole on the golf course and, of course, where the new homes were going up and how fast things seemed to be growing.

Early in their first year on Hilton Head mother and father met a fellow named Bill Cornelia. He and my father enjoyed many of the same things...

My father had occasionally taken on the duty of accompanying Bill on his various explorations of the Island. It was great fun for both of them. Hilton Head, although six years into the progress of modern development, was still an Island of uninhabited places, mysterious ruins, sand roads that often seemed to go nowhere (and frequently didn't), of untracked beaches and deep forests, exactly the kinds of places Bill and my father liked. Pop went for the sheer pleasure of it, but Bill went to record it, to catch what he could of this Island on film. This he has continued faithfully to do for low these 16 years and it is largely this unique and special view of Hilton Head Island that is the reason for this book.

Between the covers are collected the shadows that have crossed his lens within the span of his life here. What is really special about them is that there is no contrivance, no tricks with film, no special lighting effects, no hiding in specially constructed blinds to obscure the photographer from man or beast; what *is* seen here is what is here for all to see - for you as well as Bill. What is here is Hilton Head Island as it is now. This book will be out of date almost before its publication so rapid and dramatic are the changes, but it will attempt to record the Hilton Head of now while providing some insight into her past and perhaps even her future.

I well remember my first trip to the Island. I was home on leave just in from the Far East and rather than going to the house I so well knew on the shores of a Wisconsin lake, I found myself stepping off the plane in Savannah on a cool, clear, fall

morning and feeling right at home as soon as I saw my parents' smiles welcoming me back. They had just moved to the Island - Sea Pines Homebuilders (then under the guidance of Joseph Fraser) was just beginning to put the framing up on the newly poured slab. We were to stay in a house belonging to friends. It looked right down the fourteenth and then fifteenth fairways of the Ocean Golf Course. I had never stayed in a house on a golf course before, but after nearly two years in various parts of Southeast Asia and Korea it sounded awfully good to me. Until I started to look around. As the big, blue Chrysler made its way through the back roads of Georgia and then South Carolina, I began to wonder if my parents had taken leave of their senses. This country didn't look like it was doing a good job of supporting the local residents, what few there seemed to be. The bawling orange

of Joker Joe's Fireworks Stand seemed to be the main attraction between the airport and the Island.

"Look at the size of these oaks," my father said gleefully as we sped along a particularly deserted stretch of road. I did and noticed the moss hanging from them and the towering pines next to them and the more and more prevalent stretches of marshland going by and then suddenly we came to an open place in the road with a sandy beach on the right and abruptly we were on a bridge over water where we stopped for the first time since the airport. I got out to stretch my legs and look ahead to see what the hold-up was and the clean salt smell filled my lungs and two long years began to peel off and float away in the blue-green water below. The hold-up was a swing-bridge (the now absent James F. Byrnes Bridge) which was open allowing a flotilla of some 6 or 7 shrimp boats to pass through on their way to the docks at "Bennie Hudson's for unloading," as my father explained when we got on our way. We passed high over the intracoastal waterway and reached the Island. The road was straight, but not in very good repair and traffic was slow. Things still didn't look too promising along the roadsides, but everything had a sort of clean look about it. There were a few unpainted houses and several types of wooden boats along the roadsides - some on trailers, some not. As we made a long turn to head south the trees closed in and opened only to reveal the handsome entrance to Port Royal. "That's the other Plantation," they said. "There is Port Royal and Sea Pines, but that's all." The trees closed back in again and didn't stop until we arrived at a traffic circle. There we went around and headed for the beach. I liked everything I saw. The road was marked Pope Avenue and it too was mostly heavily wooded on both sides by oaks and pines and bay trees with palmettos in the low areas. There was a church and at the far end of the road just

opposite the beach a low stucco building called the Bank of Beaufort. The sun glinted off the Atlantic waves across the road and woods along the roadside thinned a bit to allow the steady ocean breeze through. Next we turned down South Forest Beach Road and drove along the ocean - just woods and sand and water beyond. On the left we passed the Adventure Inn and shortly after the William Hilton Inn. They both had a charm and style I hadn't expected, but the questions I had earlier were long gone from my mind. After the William Hilton Inn more trees and then a plywood shed in the center of the road with a man in it - nice crisp clean Sears and Roebuck grey work clothes and no hat.

"Hello, Mr. Thompson," he said with a smile. "Mr. Fraser be lookin' for you when you get home." My father thanked him for the message and drove on. More trees. Then every so often and so cleverly hidden I almost missed them, I'd see a house. I had never seen a place like this before. Homes, mostly constructed of wood stained different shades, but all natural earth tones. No yellow ones, no red ones, no blue ones. When we pulled up to our house I could hear the ocean, but I couldn't see it. I hurried behind the house to see the golf course and there it was. Emerald green deep forest on each side and at the end of "our" fairway an elevated green with a yellow flag flapping briskly in the breeze blowing off the ocean. "Well," said Pop, pride in his voice. "What do you think?" It took me a few moments to swallow the lump in my throat to answer.

That is my recollection of the first time I ever saw Hilton Head Island. I never got over it. The bright colors of the sky and marsh, the deep shadowed forests and smell of the sea, cut grass mixed with salt air, the flash of color as the cardinals and buntings and chickadees fly by and the sound of the poor-wills-widow as the sun's last light flickers out. Those impressions have stayed with me these 16 years and have become a part of the fabric of my life. I didn't come to live here with my new bride until six years later and it was then that my real education began.

Life takes on a certain rhythm on Hilton Head somehow connected to the whole stream of history, to the earliest beginnings of the place. On the planet Earth there are hundreds of thousands of islands - some inhabited, some not. Each unique in shape and size, each a host to its own environment, its own history, its own images of life. And so it is with Hilton Head. Now known across the oceans of the world as a place of great natural beauty and forgiving climate, Hilton Head joined the ranks of islands millions of years ago.

As the continental shelf formed and cooled and the earth shook itself into shape over the millions of heating and cooling years, the Island slowly took shape. The glaciers receded leaving countless tons of water, and great riverbeds behind — the Kettle Moraine country in Wisconsin formed from the leavings of the great masses of ice that retreated as the earth adjusted to its orbit and showed its broad face to the heat of the sun. The sea rose and covered the land in some cases isolating ridges of hard packed sand forming raging streams of water and shifting coastlines searching for some comfortable lasting configuration. The shelf of the great continental land mass now called North America stretched itself out to sea - along the South Carolina coast some 40 miles - calming the incoming sea - slowing the tides and gently shaping and scouring the shore.

The ceaseless wind blew and with it came life. Life in the form of dry seeds and spores and seed bearing leaves and life came by way of the sea. Husks of fruits and flotillas of sea plants washed onto the wide gentle beaches. And life came on the wings of birds in the form of stubborn burrs and sticky seeds. Some took root and the cycle of growing things began.

This formation is in sharp contrast to

the great explosions of the Sandwich Islands, the islands we now call Hawaii, and other Pacific islands, where towers of steam and ash rose thousands of feet into the air exploding in great gasps of earthfire from the ocean floor. Where layer upon layer of molten rock climbed to the surface of the sea and collided with the sunlight. Where explosion after explosion over the period of a million years shaped and molded the vertical cliffs and rolling hills and barren deserts and rainbow encrusted valleys. These islands and many others were born the same way.

Life there, both plant and animal, seems to have a tendency toward the dramatic. Plants grow that exist nowhere else on earth — birds flash with blindingly bright plumage through endless chains of sparkling sunlit days on the shore. Within sight of the sky-clear beach a mountain peak rises in Kauai that is the rainiest spot on earth. And there is even snow on the top of the towering Mauna Loa in the winter

- a short car ride from one of the world's great year 'round surfing beaches. This a land of great extremes - in birth and life - the land of the lotus eaters.

Hilton Head Island was not exploded into the world, but patiently, slowly wrested from the protecting shore - sculpted by the great salt water river now called the intra-coastal waterway, a protected body of water running the length of the east coast.

It is an almost mystical body of water formed by connected bays, rivers, and waterways and estuaries. Sometimes gentle and narrow, sometimes windblown and wide and fretted with shoals and curves - it now serves as a watery highway for pleasure cruisers and coal barges and oil tankers. The waterway is formed, from the South Carolina border to the northern part of Florida, by a chain of sea islands, some-times called the "golden chain" or the "golden isles." The chain covers over 250 miles of coastline beginning at the Santee and ending with the St. Johns River. Hilton

Captain William Hilton's ship "Adventure," as envisioned by Island artist Walter Greer

Head gradually grew to become the largest island in the chain. Over 12 miles long and up to 5 miles wide covering over 42 square miles and rising to a height of 26 feet above the sea. The Island beaches are protected from the violence of the deep sea by 40 miles of continental shelf and from the mainland by 3 short miles of open water and emerald green sea marshes. The beach formed a gentle, almost imperceptibly sloping sand flat nearly 600 feet wide at low tide comprised of a fine-grained white quartz sand, mixed with almost powdered traces of bauxite and other mineral sands. It stretched, without interruption for the full length of the Island, being only occasionally interrupted by high bluffs and streams. The land grew rich with plants of a wide variety and the first generations of the great southern trees began to take root and grow. Loblolly pine, bay, ash, sycamore, hickory, magnolia - all the giants of the sub-tropical forest grew and Hilton Head Island

took its place as a link in the "golden chain." The Island took on the shape of a shoe with the toe pointed to the southwest.

This was indeed not a volcanic beginning, but a gradual, almost gentle birth by comparison. And so too does all of the ebb and flow of the history - in fact the whole texture of the place seems to reflect this comparatively gentle start. The climate is moderate, officially called subtropical, averaging in the 60's during the winter months and the high 80's in the summer. The weather is moderated by the warm Atlantic currents and prevailing winds and will only rarely turn dark-ugly and howl a North-easter down the pipe and onto the low-lying shore.

Yet subtropical may sound like something it isn't. It really means, not quite tropical. The Island developed in a region with four very distinct seasons. Summer is very warm, with gentle ocean breezes - and high humidity. There is a fair amount of

rain in the form of low scudding clouds
blowing in on southwest winds and building
to high thunderheads by early afternoon.
At 3 or 4 pm the sky will open and drench
the land and by 6 in the evening all is fresh
and clean and clear. Fall is best described
by cool, clear days and gentle evenings. It
seldom rains at all. In winter the days are
clear, though often rain will come in the
form of a light misty drizzle and last all day.
Sometimes fog blows in from the warm
ocean mixed with cool air. Every two or three
years magic happens. The wind blows a
storm in from the northwest, moist air is
pulled in from the south and suddenly there
is snow. It usually falls in great, wet flakes
and it covers everything with a white mantle.
Nothing is more spectacular than a moss
draped oak covered with snow or the sharp
contrast of a white crest on a palmetto tree.
When it snows offices close, schools, stores,
restaurants - everything stops. People roll
in it, make snowmen, have snowball fights,

eat it...it is endlessly and ever so briefly exciting. On rare occasions it will last two or three days. The spring comes early and stays late. Warm enough to sunbathe, little rain, flowers, cloudless skies and longer and longer days. In fall the leaves do not turn dramatic colors (the sycamore does get bright yellow) but the weather changes, the air is dryer, even the smell of the place changes. Such are the seasons of the Island.

The yearly high temperature is about 75 degrees and the yearly low 55 degrees. The sun shines on the Island well over 60% of the possible time. The Island is washed and watered by nearly 50 inches of rain each year, a moderate amount by most standards, save perhaps the weather station at Death Valley. The climate is ideal for growing things. Forests grew and died and regenerated and grew again. Aside from a high bluff area at the broad north end of the island (the heel of the shoe) the land is generally flat and low in profile.

At some point in time in the dark shadows of prehistory, animals came to the Island. We don't know all of them, but we know their descendants. The native racoon, the great fox squirrel (now found only in Moss Creek Plantation just off the Island), white-tailed deer, possum, grey wolf, the coastal black bear, and the bobcat and the cougar were all familiar with Island trails. Hilton Head somehow developed a fresh water spring (now within the gates of Spanish Wells Plantation) and undoubtedly all the beasts of the forest went there for water. The vast sea marsh, a nursery for all the animals of the sea and land, formed over half the Island. Life abounded there. Oysters, shrimp, crabs, clams and mussels all found homes in the soft black nutritious "plough mud," the basic stuff of the marsh. And the water flowed in streams, part salt and part fresh into and off of the Island. Ponds and swamps were formed and black-water pools turned deep reflecting onyx by the tannin leached from the bark of the cypress trees' rotted detrium on the bottom. Out of these places came the green-eyed alligator, and the red skink and blue-tail racer and the magical, many colored chameleon and the snake. Oh yes, there were and are snakes on the Island, now more shy and retiring than ever. Most all of the snakes common to the coastal shores of North American could be found here, and turtles. The marsh and the subtropical forests and plants brought birds, too. The deep forest rang with the trumpeting call of the great wild turkey, the whistle of the southern quail and the cooing of the grey dove. And there were bright red cardinals, the flashy little painted buntings—over 250 species could be found at one season or another during the year. There were and are shore birds, too. Terns and gulls and sandpipers, tippits, pelicans in long lazy lines and egrets and ibises and cranes and herons. In each area of the Island every form of life made its own way and found it to be a generous and kindly host. And with the ebb and flow of the tides the scene was set and the Island shaped like a shoe, abundant in life forms and green with plants and trees, waited patiently for the entrance of man.

Man came. We don't know why. Probably in search of food, or safety, or both. Early man made the first discovery of Hilton Head beyond the scope of our vision into the past. He was probably less of a hunter than a gatherer. Among the clear evidences we have of the earliest man on the Island are the ancient and mute shell rings found in two places, one in the Sea Pines Forest Preserve and the other on the side of Squire Pope Road on the north end of the Island. They tell us little, but they tell us that some-one was here and that they wished for some reason, perhaps ceremonial, to arrange many, many oyster shells in a circular pattern. We know from carbon dating, the materials used to build the rings are some 4000 years old. Recently a group of historians unearthed, during the development of some condominiums, the shell of one ancient dug-out canoe over 2000 years old, so we know now that these early people came to the Island in boats. Their tools, stone grinders and arrow heads tell us they used the plants and animals here for food and shelter. We can at least see the shadows, the dimmest outlines of the first Islanders, the first discoverers. This Island must have provided its own protection for them with the moderate climate requiring little in the way of clothing. Their shelter must have been made from the plant growth; there are no caves or rocks to hide among. They fed on the land - the fruits and berries and the oysters and crabs. Perhaps they caught fish, probably shore or pond dwellers like flounder, and brim and spot-tail bass. The sea beyond was not their world though they must have seen the great herds of porpoise feeding near the shore and watched the ex-plosive splash of the great manta rays in the sound, and seen the water birds over

the great cobia in the narrows of the broad creek in the middle of the Island. They may have hunted or even trapped small animals, perhaps even the wily black bear for their winter robes and meat.

We do not know their names, but little by little as the mists of time pull away some Indian names have come to us...the Calibogue, the Escamacu, although I know relatively little about them. They were coastal Indians, however, and we now live on land that at one time was indeed Indian territory — by right of possession — the Island of the Indians that could hold it.

In the year 1521 a Spanish explorer named Pedro de Quexos reported sighting a promontory on the coastline as he sailed up the coast of Georgia and Carolina searching for new lands and treasure. This high ground is clearly the land that rises 26 feet above the shore in what is now Port Royal Plantation. It is likely he sailed up the broad sound, found a favorable anchorage and became the first European to set foot on the Island. It became marked on early Spanish charts as a place to find fresh water — essential to the long voyages these intrepid seafarers made in their small ships. The Island was graced with a fresh water pool located almost at the waters' edge on the inland side. The water ran deep near the shore and it was a protected anchorage, thus an ideal spot for a rest. It is very likely that the first men to set foot on the Island came for much the same reasons modern visitors do; rest, food, and shelter. The fresh water pool - a slow seepage type of spring - is still functioning within the confines of Spanish Wells Plantation. University of South Carolina archeological digs there have uncovered fragments of armor, coins and parts of swords traceable to Spanish origin.

By the year 1562, the Island had seen many Spanish ships and crews stop at the well site for water, fresh game and what fruits and vegetables they could gather. The shoreline there, although now flanked by

Port Royal Plantation - Looking toward Port Royal Sound

Remains of the steam cannon at Port Royal Plantation

some of the Island's most elegant homes at Spanish Wells, appears very much the same as it must have to those courageous Spanish sailor men. The Spanish undoubtedly encountered the Island Indians here and possibly traded for some goods the Indians could provide, perhaps skins, corn, nuts and berries. This year brought a new group of visitors to the Island's shores: the French. A boat full of Huguenots led by Captain Jean Ribaut came up the sound to the Island seeking a place to colonize and set up lives far from the persecution of an intolerant Catholic France. They christened the sound they entered as "Port Royale," now known, of course, as Port Royal Sound. The term "Port Royale" really was a general sort of area reference, just as "Santa Elena," the Spanish designation for the Island, was meant not just for the Island, but for the waters and islands surrounding Hilton Head. The French came, but did not stay here; they moved further up the sound seeking greater protection from the sea and Spanish eyes, finally choosing a site on Parris Island. There they established the settlement they called "Charlesfort," and had the honor of being the first protestant settlement in what is now the United States. They were continually harrassed by the Spanish and the native coastal Escamacu Indians and after nearly 50 years of skirmishes bowed to the Spanish and took what little they had and disappeared into the mists of time. Getting started on the Carolina coast was not going to be easy.

In 1662 King Charles II of England made a grant of land - Carolina - to eight royal favorites called thereafter Lords Proprietors. This was done to create incentive for the English lords to explore the new world more fully and to, as a consequence, expand the British Empire. It worked. This grant and others like it helped open a period of English exploration and colonization along the full sweep of the Atlantic coastline from the Virginias to the northern coastline

of Florida. A group of Barbados planters commissioned a popular young sea captain named William Hilton to explore the coast and report on the possibilities of the new land. Commanding a three-masted ship called the "Adventure", he set forth from Spikes Bay on August 10, 1663, and sailed north catching sight of the continental coastline some sixteen days later. He entered the waters of Port Royal Sound and after entertaining some Indians on board ship and receiving some rather discomforting information about the presence of Spaniards and a few captured Englishmen in the area, they sailed up and down the myriad waterways-parlayed with both Indians and Spanish soldiers and managed to free a few of the English castaways. This done, they sailed to the open waters of Port Royal Sound and explored the Island.

They walked on the Island and took a close look at it. In his "A Relation of the Discovery Lately Made on the Coast of Florida" (all the southern coastal region was generally called that), Hilton provided a clear picture of the Island - "The lands," he said, "are laden with large, tall oaks, walnut and bayes, except facing the Sea, it is most pines tall and good." He commented that the soil looked rich and fertile and said, "The Indians plant in the worst land because they couldn't cut down the timber in the best, yet have plenty of corn, pumpkins, watermelons, musk melons: although the land be overgrown with weeds through their laziness, yet they have two or three crops of corn a year. The country abounds with grapes, large figs, and peaches and the woods with deer, conie (racoons), turkeys, quails,

curlews, plovers, teal, herons; and as the Indians say in winter with swans, geese, cranes, ducks and mallard, and innumerable of other water fowls, whose names we do not know." He concluded that "the ayr is clear and sweet, the country very pleasant and delightful."

In earlier days the French had called the Island "Ile de la Riviere Grande," or Island of the Broad River, but subsequent to William Hilton's adventure it began to show on some English charts as Hilton Head Island. He had been impressed by the high ground at the north end (now in Port Royal Plantation) and commented on the distinctive "headland" at the entrance to Port Royal Sound. Three years after Captain Hilton's discovery of the Island, Captain Robert Sanford reached Hilton Head and put ashore the first English settler of Carolina, Dr. Henry Woodward. He lived on the Island with the Indians until he was captured by the Spanish and sent to prison at St. Augustine. He eventually found his way back to Hilton Head and finally settled in Charleston. The Island quietly rested under the control of the Indians and was only occasionally interrupted by Spanish ships putting in for supplies.

The Indians became more adept at trading and required more for the fish, dried meats, corn and nuts the seamen wanted. They demanded beads, axes, metal knives, and warm cloth. The English crown in 1698 granted "Hilton Head Island" to one John

Bayley - he apparently did not discourage the newest appellation for the Island "Bayley's Barony." He apparently didn't do much "baroning" however, and it wasn't until 19 years later in 1717 on the 10th of December that Colonel John ("Tuscarora Jack") Barnwell received the first recorded land grant on Hilton Head Island: some 1000 acres later known as Myrtle Bank Plantation in the area now known as Hilton Head Plantation. He became the Island's first English settler nearly half a century after William Hilton's voyage. The Island became known for a time as Trenches Island as the result of Bayley's appointment of one Alexander Trench as his Carolina property agent and collector of tax fees. It seems it has always been thus - even poor old "Tuscarora Jack" had to pay taxes.

For a long period of time from 1717 to nearly 1729 Hilton Head still remained the province of the wildlife and Indians. Although ownership of land increased, through land grants and even land sales, land ownership on Hilton Head was largely a speculative business. Colonel John Barnwell's purchase of 1000 acres of "prime Island land" was simply a speculative buy, the type of investment not unknown today on Hilton Head. It was not likely that he considered moving to the Island from his lovely bay front home in Beaufort which rested on the site of the present courthouse.

It wasn't until the 1720's that some

homesteads began to appear on the scene. There along the quiet banks of the Broad River the first Island plantations began to take shape. There is little record of them, or evidence. The houses were wooden structures, generally one story with a few out buildings. They raised corn and rye and garden vegetables and melons. There were a few farm animals and horses, and the larger farms had a few slaves. These were not the grand plantations of the Antebellum South, but basic, hard-working little homesteads that needed much attention and protection.

The Yemassee Indians, encouraged by a Scotsman of an earlier time to come up from Florida, moved into the area and held fast. They were resourceful and clever, able to trade with a white man in the morning and hunt him down in the afternoon. The period between the early 1700's and into the 1730's is known as the time of the Yemassee wars. Skull Creek probably derived its name (so one legend has it) from being called 'Skulk' Creek because the Indians were known to hide in ambush along the shores waiting for planters to glide by with boatloads of food or grain. It was the site of many a bloody struggle - and eventually took on the appellation Skull Creek - still used today.

Names like Lancelot Bland, Captain John Gascony, Christopher Dawson have

drifted down as names of men who inhabited the shores of Broad Creek during the treacherous days of the Indian wars. There are many legends about these early days, about Indian uprisings, heroic deeds and desperate nights of capture, escape and death. The finger of land at the tip of neighboring Daufuskie is named "Bloody Point" as evidence of such long-lost tales. Legend has it a group of young planters gathered together and stole across the sound in the dead of a moonless night and slaughtered an encampment of Indian women and children left defenseless by the braves who had gone out on a raiding party. The sound ran red with Indian blood that night and ever after that spot has been called Bloody Point. The mists of time obscure much of these early days; men were too busy going about the business of survival to put much of their experience on record.

But the climate and the fertile soil of the Low Country drew more and more people and those people experimented and challenged the elements with new techniques and crops and as their farms grew they became known as "plantations" - really another name for communities. Slaves were bought at the Savannah and Charlestown markets and brought to work on the farms, and slowly, slowly, the sea island plantation culture began to take shape. Cotton, rice, indigo, corn and sugar cane all became important crops - crops that would for many decades make the south strong and, yes, rich, too.

It wasn't until 1790 that Mr. William Elliot boasted the first crop of what was to become known the world over as Sea Island Cotton on the old Barnwell grant that he called "Myrtle Bank Plantation." This long fibered cotton was considered to be stronger, softer and generally the finest cotton in the world. He maintained a combination of factors caused it to grow. First he said he "selected only the finest seeds from the best plants of each crop" and he and his neighbor William Seabrook adopted a clever method of fertilizing - using the rich black marsh mud one year and ground oyster shell the next. This alternate schedule of fertilizing kept the soil rich and productive. The low-lying fields were converted to rice growing by creating small plots or "tasks" as they were often called. This was done with the cotton fields as well, but these were divided into somewhat larger quarter acre squares 105 by 105 feet. A slave was assigned to each "task" and he or she remained responsible for that area or several such areas all their lives. As the plantation grew so did the homes they built and the lands they kept. Land was continually being sold or traded to increase the size of the plantation - the larger it got, the more money it could make - the

more slaves it could afford - the larger it could grow. It was a cycle known all over the south.

Whenever possible the plantation house would be located near a river or stream, on high ground - where the cool refreshing breeze could get at it. Water was the major means of transportation, so proximity to navigable water was a necessity. In the early days everything was done right on the plantation. There were tanneries where hides could be made into leather, shoe makers' shops, blacksmith and carpenter areas, cook houses (often separate from the main house), and all the buildings and equipment needed to deal with the crops. Whitney's cotton gin was of no use on the fine, long-fibered Sea Island cotton; only foot operated roller gins could be used. A slave might be assigned the chore of pedaling the gin for hours at a time - first on one foot then the other. It was exhausting, tedious work. They eventually learned to apply the horse to this arduous task. Because of the length of the staple (or strand), the cotton was always packed by hand with the packer standing right in the suspended bag. Frequently there were looms and spinning wheels - allowing cloth to be made right on the plantation for the workers and owners alike. There were mills for grinding corn and as sugar cane became an important crop, grinders for the cane and giant boil-

ing-off pots.

The houses became much improved by the discovery of "tabby" as a building material. The builders of that day found that by burning crushed oyster shells and mixing this char with more shells and sand and water and mud in various proportions, a thick pasty concrete of sorts resulted. This could be packed between wooden frames and used for foundations and walls. Tabby walls were commonly nearly about a foot thick and were both sound and wind proof. Most of the plantation houses of Hilton Head were made of tabby and the remnants of a few can be seen today; the last vestiges of Elliott's Myrtle Bank Plantation houses at the north end of the Island are now washed by the tides of Port Royal sound off Dolphin Head. Some of the tabby walls of Cotton Hope can be seen standing in a farmer's field on the north end of the Island just off Squire Pope Road. The most prominent of the tabby ruins is in the Baynard Park preserved within Sea Pines Plantation at the south end of the Island. The houses were not architecturally handsome but solid and not greatly ornamented. They were functional houses quite warm in winter and surprisingly cool in summer.

Today on Hilton Head and in other parts of the Low Country a stucco material with oyster shell in it is commonly used to provide a tabby look to some homes, but it is no longer used in its original form, partly because the actual proportions and methods of making it have been lost to modern builders.

As the various families settled into the Island, time passed. Land was traded and sold to newcomers, left to children, split and redefined and little by little antebellum Hilton Head emerged. A chapel was built, called the Zion Chapel of Ease as a part of St. Luke's Parish in 1767. A wooden church stood on the site now just a graveyard at the corner of Highway #278 and Matthews Drive. It was the place of worship for prominent Island families. The Barksdale, Baynard, Chaplin, Devant, Fripp, Kirk, Matthews, Pope, Storey and Webb families all worshipped at the Zion Chapel of Ease. A lovely story surrounds this chapel. In 1833 two silver chalices made by Bernard Brothers of London were given to the church. When the Civil War struck the Island, chaos prevailed and in the burning and looting that followed the silver chalices were lost. They resurfaced in the early 1900's in a Philadelphia hock shop - black and tarnished beyond recognition. They were purchased and polished and cleaned revealing the inscription "Zion Chapel Hilton Head." Realizing these were not casual silver goblets but religious articles, the owner returned them to St. Helena's Church in Beaufort. There they rested until 1964 when the new St. Luke's Episcopal Church was

completed and they were returned to their Hilton Head home once again.

A typical plantation had up to 2000 acres of land attributed to it. There would be the main house, not too decorous but spacious and solid, clusters of out buildings for dealing with crops and livestock, and several rows of small slave cabins to house the working staff of the place. An active plantation might have as many as 100 to 150 slaves. It was, generally, a self-sufficient, busy place. As the plantation culture matured here. The patterns of life smoothed out.

Typically the owners would live on the Island during the fall, winter and spring months and move to the "up country" in the hot, mosquito-ridden summers, leaving the plantation to the care of an overseer and the slaves. Island plantation owners typically had second homes (usually working plantations as well) in places like; Augusta, Camden, Columbia, and even as far away as Macon. By inheritance, by sale, by gift, by grant, the land unspoken for on the Island got spoken for. Names like Lawton, Leamington, Gardner, Seabrook, Coggins Point, Braddocks' Point, Fish Haul, Cherry Hill, Spanish Wells and Shipyard, all became places on the Island, names of plantations that participated in the quiet, sleepy but relentless subjugation of the land to the plow. And then came the Revolution. It happened here, too; certainly it did. It is recorded that many of the Islanders were rebels and thus the objects of at least some amount of interest to the Loyalists and British troops on the mainland. Although no major battle or war was known to be fought here - there were skirmishes and burnings. As the battles raged elsewhere in the country, an order came down in the fall of 1781 for the British forces to muster and march from Charlestown to Savannah and burn out "all known rebels" on the way. It was about that time that the Talbird home was torched (probably by local Tories). Hard

feelings followed and more trouble ensued. Charles Devant, a prominent Island planter and owner of Marshland and Folly Field Plantations, was killed on his own land at the head of Broad Creek by a Tory captain from Daufuskie. This resulted in a group of Islanders (patriots all) gathering together and calling themselves the "Bloody Legion." These stalwart lads crossed the Calibogue Sound at night and laid waste a number of Tory homes, not to mention the man thought to be responsible for Charles Devant's murder. Today an historical marker at the intersection of 278 and Matthews Drive marks the spot where Devant fell. He is buried nearby in the Zion Chapel of Ease Cemetery. Judging from the amount of historical energy expended on this incident, it is probably fair to say Hilton Head Island was not in the mainstream of the Revolution, but certainly was not untouched.

The only other remarkable incident with the British occurred much later when on August 22, 1813, the British landed on the Island "in force" and burned most of the homes that were built on deep water property. Obviously these were easy targets for them to reach and easy to escape from as well. Generally speaking, however, life went on peacefully on the Island until the Civil War. In that period cotton became King. The Stoney family became the most powerful family on the Island and at one point owned a vast majority of the land through one branch of the family or other. The great Baynard house (now the previously referred to ruin in the Baynard Park at Sea Pines Plantation) was built of tabby around 1793 by Captain Jack Stoney as a part of Braddock's Point Plantation. This house remained in the Stoney family until the fateful night in the late 1830's when William Edings Baynard entered into a high stakes poker game. Legend has it the game was played in the little wooden house in Bluffton called the "Card House," still used as a private

residence today. When the game ended, Baynard owned the great Braddock's Point Plantation; house, dock, land, slaves and all. Some say he got it all with a pair of Kings. I can tell you from personal experience poker hasn't improved much over these last 150 years. He ultimately owned Spanish Wells, Muddy Creek as well, not to mention Buckingham over on the mainland. He obviously knew more about the plantation

business than just poker - undoubtedly a necessary skill. He was buried in the Baynard Mausoleum in the Zion Chapel of Ease Cemetary. The mausoleum is the oldest surviving antebellum structure on the Island. Although long since looted and no longer in use in its original capacity, the mausoleum stands solidly against weather and time, lending witness to the solidity and success of Islanders of another time. It's odd that the houses of the living are gone and only the house of the dead remains to

remind us of the grand times long past.

Plantation life reached a fine level of existence before the Civil War. By 1860 there were some 24 operating plantations on the Island. There were long hard months of planting, endless days of loading and unloading supplies on the plantation docks and there was singing and happiness too, and parties. Feasts consisted of quarts - no, gallons - of raw and cooked oysters, crab boils, roasted and boiled shrimp and fried flounder. Smoked hams, cornbread, grits with melted cheese, and fried green tomatoes and boiled eggs and biscuits. The delightful "She-Crab" soup emerged as a local delicacy; made from sweet fresh milk, herbs and spices, plenty of red pepper and only the meat and roe from egg-bearing female crabs. The Island delicacy of crab cakes was a perfected art by this time. There were riding contests and cookouts and "Gander pullings" where the young men of the family rode the fastest horse past a greased goose handing upside down from a high branch. The object was to pull the head off the goose without slowing down. Fortunately for the goose, greasy and squirming and never a still target, only the finest riders ever succeeded. If they did accomplish the grisly task there was much celebrating and (pardon the pun) the goose was cooked.

I have mentioned - but only slightly-the fact that slaves were brought to the Island to work these sprawling farm communities called plantations. They were brought from the slave markets of Charlestown and Savannah. They price for the buying and selling of slaves was predicated on the price of indigo, cotton and rice. These records from a southern slave market show the price was not cheap. "Boys 5 ft. $850 - $950. Young women any size in fit condition $800 - $1000. Best men 18 to 25 yr. old $1200 - $1300." When Island land was selling for around $18 per acre this shows that much of the value of a plantation had to be measured in the community of people that made it run.

Repellent as the product was - it is a fact of our American South - slavery was the keystone of the rural southern economy. The Black heritage of the Island belongs to the "Gullah" natives. It is largely believed the blacks that were brought to this part of the south (from Charleston to Savannah) were brought from Angola or "Gola," a country of West Africa and part of Lower Guinea. The term "Gullah" derived from these regional references and has stayed with the blacks of the Island to this day. Further evidence of the "Gullah" origins has been substantiated by study of the Gullah basketry and speech patterns in recent years. The people were brought in squalid ships, carted down long bumpy roads to the river and brought over to the Island in chains. It was the Gullah men who cut the trees, pulled the stumps and cleared the fields. It was the Gullah men who planted the cotton and cleaned the weeds from the corn rows. And it was the Gullah men, women and children who pulled the long sacks on their backs through the cotton fields placing clump after clump of snowy Sea Island cotton in the bag until it was nearly too heavy to move. They lived in rudimentary houses at best and had little of their own. Hilton Head was known as a "hard workin'" place, but also not a bad place because it wasn't too cold too often, and there was the wonderful creek and all the life the sea could give and fertile soil for your own little vegetable patch. Certain unique characteristics have merged from these people that were forged in African soil, and hardened by the life slavery forced them to live.

The Gullah black has historically never taken the role of aggressor but in their slow, painful struggle they have developed a spiritual strength which can be the envy of any other ethnic group. There is always an optimism about them, a positive bent - and there is a strong sense of sharing and

giving and an innate sense of humor. Threaded through these basic qualities is a deep sense of religion - and in the early days a sense of spiritualism mixed together with fear and mystery brought from the dark corners of the African continent. Voodoo was practiced in the dark of night under the towering trees, the fires lighting the hanging moss and lending a ghastly air.

I know little of these things - but I know there are those who steadfastly maintain there are still some voodoo practitioners on the Island, unknown and unseen. There is a great reverence for the dead in the Gullah mind, a respect for age and wisdom. Graveyards are special places, carefully kept and maintained. It is customary to place pieces of broken pottery or a favorite piece of glassware or cup on the grave to be touched by no-one ever after. In the little cemetery at Harbour Town in Sea Pines you can see homemade concrete headstones with whole plates pressed into them as a loving, gentle gesture to the departed. In DuBose Heyward's story "The Half Pint Flask," he tells a ghostly tale of a northern visitor to a Carolina Sea Island who fancies a rare half pint bottle left for generations on a Gullah grave. Although warned to leave it alone, he removes it, only to be haunted by the deadly "plat-eye" ghost who protects the Gullah graves. Finally in a terrifying scene he is forced to flee the Island. Maybe just a story, maybe not. Traditionally people who drown are buried in the marsh because of a superstition the sea must claim its dead or claim a new victim.

The Gullah dialect is unlike any other language anywhere else in the world. It is a melodic, soft rolling combination of Old English and African. It is not a "pidgin" language, but a true English dialect and if spoken exclusively almost impossible for the untutored ear to comprehend. There is wisdom and wit woven deeply into the language. One of the choicest Gullah idioms is "oomon iz soatoam ting" or as Shakespeare said "frailty thy name is woman." In Gullah, when one is worried or troubled, "greebunce gottum." To take an oath, "possit your word." To take it easy, "saddlin' along." To be off schedule or late, "outtuh 'e runnin." To make a judgement of someone unworthy of trust, "da gal him 'long de rood 'en a nubbah study 'bout nuttin." To be a slave in the deep south, "to be sole down de ribbuh."

The sly wit and deep humor of the Gullah people was brought to public light by a young Atlanta newspaperman named Joel Chandler Harris. He popularized the Gullah folk-tales he heard while in the low country. The resulting Uncle Remus tales including Br'er Rabbit and Br'er Fox and Br'er Bear and such famous tales as the "Tarbaby Story" are among the world's most delightful folk tales. It is still thought they had an origin in African folk tales but they became special, relating the slave experience and indomitable spirit of the Gullah people. Typical of the humor and agility of mind the Gullah language describes is this boy's description of a jackass, "Oh, de jackass-'e plain to see - 'e look same lak a mule only mo 'so." Although now become less and less prevalent, the Gullah language still persists, a part of the Sea Island heritage.

The Gullah people also love to worship and sing. This was done in the praise houses,simple wooden buildings with rough benches to sit on and a few high windows for ventilation. The music came from African rhythm and soared into unique spiritual singing, often with movement and repeated phrases:

I know moon-rise, I know star-rise
    lay dis body down
I walk in de moonlight, I walk in
        de daylight
    lay dis body down
I'll walk in the graveyard, I'll walk
        through de graveyard
    lay dis body down
I'll lie in de graveyard and stretch out
        my arms
    lay dis body down
I go to d' judgement in 'de evenin' of
        de day
    when I lay dis body down
And my soul and your soul will
        meet in de day
    when I lay dis body down

Deep words, moving phrases, often praying for peace in life and death - this music floated in the Island air and still does on many a Saturday or Sunday night.

So, the stage is set. The people are in place. The clouds had gathered by 1860 - all over the south. The south's most wrenching, life shaking event was about to take place. The Civil War. It affected the Island as it did the rest of the nation. The men of the Island were organized into a Confederate militia and their first act was to construct an earth-work fortification at the entrance to Port Royal Sound. They cut palmetto logs (impervious to rot, they thought) and placed them upright, filling in between with soil. They dug a moat around the outside of it and built a few gun emplacements inside, trained on the sound. They named it Fort Walker. South Carolina seceded from the Union and Thomas

40

Drayton of the Island militia was put in command of Fort Walker. The men searched the harbor for enemy ships; they saw nothing. They practiced with the guns, drilled, patrolled the Island and took to having lazy evenings and mornings at home. For seven long months nothing happened.

Then, on a cool November 7, 1861, the dawn rose on the most awesome sight any of these gentle Island people had ever seen. Coming into Port Royal Sound on silent

white wings was a Union fleet of nearly 46 ships. Fifteen gunships and thirty-one transports, the largest naval force ever gathered in American waters. Under President Abraham Lincoln's orders to blockade southern ports and close off southern trade and coastal transportation, this force aimed its guns on Fort Walker and Fort Beauregard opposite Hilton Head at Bay Point. It was an odd and sad quirk of fate that the captain of one of the gunships, the "Pocahontas," was

Percival Drayton, brother of Thomas Drayton, the commander of Fort Walker. The sight of that mighty attack force must have struck cold fear and hatred into the hearts of the men so used to the peaceful life on the Island. The warships formed a large circle and sailed first past Fort Walker and then past Fort Beauregard, firing withering salvos as they passed within range off shore. A small consignment of Confederate ships, four in number, moored near the Fort, scattered. In less than five hours the 150 guns of the Union fleet had silenced the 40 guns of Fort Walker. When the Union force of 12,000 men landed they found the Fort deserted and, except for the confused Gullah people that remained, the Island was empty of white men or women.

In all, the Union troops lost 8 dead and 23 wounded, the Confederates some 59

Oyster gatherers in the winter sea marsh

killed or wounded. With the war only six months old, Hilton Head had become a Union stronghold, and so it remained until the surrender at Appomattox on April 9, 1865. Walker was renamed Fort Wells to honor Gideon Wells, U.S. Secretary of the Navy, and Fort Beauregard became Fort Seward. The plantation house at Coggins Point, once the home of the Pope family, became the home for a succession of Union officers who commanded the Island fort-ification. To secure the Island a series of earthwork forts was built - including Fort Mitchell, Fort Sherman and Fort Howell. They lined the north end of the Island from Skull Creek to the Atlantic Ocean. The earthen remains of Forts Walker and Sherman are today part of Port Royal Plantation and Fort Mitchell, somewhat restored, rests overlooking Skull Creek in Hilton Head Plantation.

It has always fascinated me to think that there, only a short march away, was Savannah and to the north, Charleston - yet no major effort was made to recapture the Island by the Confederates. The first (but not last) Yankee invasion of the Island seemed unimportant to the Confederates and with the exception of a few (poorly documented) guerilla attacks on supplies and boats, little activity of a warlike nature transpired. Other more subtle changes took place. While the officers and even wives took target practice on the beach and the troops learned about snakes and alligators and the pleasures of an afternoon fishing in the creek, the Gullah people were busy developing a new sort of life for themselves. While some took care of the Federals they began to measure time in a different way.

The invasion of the Federal troops was known as the "gunshoot" and for years after they reckoned events "before the gunshoot" and "after the gunshoot." The invasionary force under the command of Commodore S.F. DuPont had captured Beaufort and the blacks helped to ransack and plunder the

The new bridge replaces the old

fine homes that were there. High carnival
was held on Hilton Head as well, but only
briefly. The freed men feasted on the turkey
and pigs and larders of the plantations, but
soon retreated to their homes and gradually
developed their own "after the gunshoot"
style of living. This style could be called sub-
sistence living of a high order. Gardens were
expanded, the fine horses and pigs were
often allowed to roam free and unclaimed,

and men spent more time on the river honing the fine skills of oystering, shrimping, crabbing and fishing. Unknowingly, subtly the life patterns took on tinges of the new south. The Island, a Union stronghold with an independent Gullah community, true to its earliest traditions, took shape. Even at that dark time in our nation's history the forces were at work shaping the Island of today.

At the site of Fort Walker a city grew up. A city of some 50,000 souls - men, women and children. Yes - 50,000! Enlisted men, both soldiers and sailors, comprised the bulk of this population, seasoned with a few Yankee tradesmen and what was probably a colorful assortment of misfits and characters sidelined by the war. The hardpacked sand main street was called "Sutler's Row" (a sutler was a person who followed troops to sell food, drink and "the usual favors" to military men). It soon became known as "Robbers' Row" by the men who learned the price of a drink on Hilton Head was high, very high. I'm forced here to repeat - things ever stay the same.

Herein rose the Island's first high-rise hotel, - The Port Royal House catering to enlisted men, visiting war correspondents, wives, and ladies on "errands of mercy." Not unlike modern promotional exaggerations were the ads for the Sea Island Hotel, one of two others besides the Port Royal House. "The Sea Island Hotel," they said, "rivals any of the fine hostelries at Newport." The Island's first paper, a weekly, was published here by one Joseph Sears who was also the postmaster. He called it "The New South" and charged $1.00 per line for advertising. A lesser sheet was also published for a short time by some rival journalists called the "Palmetto Herald" but it didn't last. Robber's Row sported a butcher shop (also sold whiskey there), an ice house, 2 bookstores, jewelry shops, dry goods stores, a theatre with 1000 seats, and a barber shop, not to mention 4 restaurants. The theater was graced at least twice with traveling productions from New York City.

Not far from Fort Walker was Mitchelville, a sort of squalid tent city, almost a refugee camp housing thousands of freedmen who fled to the Island to escape Confederate wrath on the mainland. It was built under the watchful eyes of General Ormsby Mitchel who did a fine job of maintaining some semblance of order. Unfortunately he died of yellow fever before his term on the Island was over. Generally, officers lived well and comfortably in houses either built or borrowed, furnished with items taken freely from the plantations of the Island and surrounding mainland communities.

It can be said the Island served the Union troops well and was an ideal fueling stop and repair depot. But when the war ended the troops hurriedly went home, mustering out on the parade grounds of Fort Walker. Of course, with the troops went the sutlers and by 1870 there was little left of the boom-depot town known as "Robber's Row."

Another era began. The era of the native Islanders. During the time between the end of the Civil War (1866) and the building of the Byrnes Bridge 90 years later, three generations of Hilton Head blacks grew up and lived their lives here - uninterrupted by the drastic changes that were occurring on the mainland. The big plantation houses slowly caved in, pirated and picked at by Islanders who needed materials to repair or build their own homes. The former slaves couldn't bring themselves to move into the big houses but felt no sorrow at slowly tearing them down. Most of the fine furniture was taken north by the soldiers so that little remained except the land. A few northerners stayed. A missionary society located in the state of Connecticut sent a few single young ladies down to the Island to teach the black children. In letters since discovered by relatives (now Islanders themselves) one of the teachers talks of her

love of the children and kindness of the Gullah people to her. In her book of letters titled "Dear Sister," published by the Beaufort Book Company, young Eliza Ann Summers gives a clear and telling picture of her pupils. "Such a ragged, destitute set of children you never saw, they do seem so grateful to us. There is not a day passes but they bring us a present of a few eggs or some sweet potatoes, but usually oysters. I have told you about them in my other letters how nice they are. We do not seem to get tired of them at all. We cook them so many different ways. We have stewed oysters, oysters fried in meal, which are splendid, they taste almost exactly like scallops. Then we fry them in flour, have oyster pot pie and oyster pie like chicken pie with a thick crust." She talked about the Island too as it appeared to her in 1867. "We went on the beach for eight miles and a beautiful ride it was too. Coney Island beach is not to be compared with it. On one side of us is the broad ocean,

on the other nothing but forests of pine and
palmetto trees, then such beautiful birds
- and we saw a large bald-headed eagle and
an eagle's nest." Her Island in that magically
peaceful year after the war must have been
a rare beautiful place indeed. There were
a few stragglers, of course, mostly Yankees;
Eliza did comment that the only white Rebel
was the postmaster at the time of her tenure
on the Island. The Gullah farms grew; they
produced their own potatoes, some rice,
tomatoes, melon, corn - whatever was
needed to live. The boll weevil took over
the cotton and the fields were turned over to
wild plants and garden plots. The fine
horses were generally allowed to roam free
and after several generations evolved
slightly shorter legs and broader hooves and
shaggy coats and were called "marsh
tackies." Some were caught for training and
farming; most were allowed to run free. The
domestic plantation hogs escaped and ran
wild. They adapted to their new freedom.
They grew long coats of coarse hair, the legs
lengthened and the tusks appeared and the
Island wild pig roamed the woods, perhaps
the most dangerous, ill-tempered wild
animal present.

    The Gullahs developed their own
cultural pattern; the leaders became the
men who developed the skills necessary for
survival but the community, though closely
knit, was not formally organized. It was told
to me a long time ago by one Island native
that the most respected and revered man
was the boat-builder. He held the key to
gathering food from the marshes and creeks
and to getting on and off the Island. Boats
built here on Hilton Head were typical of
the lowcountry cypress bateau: flat
bottomed, broad beamed, and solid, with
a flat transom made of one piece of wood
if possible. Nothing was measured except
by eye. Natural oils in the wood protected it
and kept it water tight. Basket weaving and
net making became fine arts and part of
the mosaic of the lowcountry crafts and skills

Palmetto Dunes beach front - showing Mariner's Inn, Captain's Walk and Hyatt Hotel

Hilton Head Island shoreline - Looking northeast

that developed during the time. The Gullah basket is truly a thing of great beauty. The women learned to make the basic material from chord or marsh grass mixed with pinestraw for color and wrapped into ropes with split palmetto fronds. A good basket weaver could fashion a basket so tight it would hold water. Over the years they evolved a countless variety of lovely patterns and shapes. Gullah baskets can still be found along the roadside vendor stands on the Island and in great numbers just on the north side of Charleston on the coast road. There is no written history of this period - it is locked in the memory of the few families left who lived on the last shining edges of the sunset of that peaceful time of the Islands' existence.

The idyl was slightly disturbed about 1902. The government still owned the 803 acres that had once been Fort Walker and "Robber's Row" and realizing we were approaching the Twentieth Century characteristically decided it was time to be armed for it. There was some official concern that the Spanish might decide to invade again and further deductions seemed to identify Hilton Head Island as a sort of hot spot for Spanish invasion. The lack of Spanish presence from the mid-1500's did not seem to have much impact on government strategists.

Remaining consistent in both concept and execution of the defense plan, a new weapon was decided upon and Fort Walker would be the perfect site. Thus, for a period of time the Island calm was shattered with hammers and saws and horsecarts and barges of brass fittings until finally it took shape - America's first steam cannon! The concept was simple - fire up the boiler with wood, create a high head of steam, release it instantly into the barrel and blam! War. It was decided it needed to be tried before the Spanish arrived. On a cool spring morning, wood was brought and a monstrous fire was built. The steam co-operated

54

Shipyard Racquet Club and Marriott Hotel

and was released upon order into the barrel. Blam! The projectile (non-explosive) carried across Port Royal Sound landing in a heavily wooded section of Bay Point. Once there it set off a substantial forest fire causing great concern and embarrassment to everyone involved. It is also thought the gun might have done some irreparable damage to itself after the gaseous explosion and was found unsafe to use again without major repairs. Thus, though it is seldom spoken of in the hallowed halls of the Pentagon, the steam cannon of Hilton Head, one of only two ever built, was dismantled and sold for scrap in the year 1917. The remains of this ingenious weapon of distinction are still to be seen by visiting Port Royal Plantaion.

Not willing to leave well enough alone, the troops returned about 1916 to a temporary barracks set up to house a small contingent of military men assigned to fend off any German submarines that might find the Island a choice target. They stayed blissfully on the beach until Armistice Day, November 11, 1918, when they dispersed. While I'm on this line of military activity on Hilton Head, I may as well follow it out. During World War II a group of Marines came to the Island and lived at the base of Leamington Lighthouse on Bass Head Beach. This area is now enclosed within an undeveloped area of Palmetto Dunes. They lived in wooden barracks built for the

purpose of housing the troops. The area was variously known as Camp McDougal and Camp Dilling. (The military has a penchant for naming things.) They manned along with the Coast Guard the Leamington Light which was the only lighthouse on the Island at that time. It was used as a range marker for troop exercises and a marine navigational beacon until 1948 when the installation was closed down. The two charming lighthouse keepers' cottages were eventually moved to Harbour Town in Sea Pines and house respectively Signe's World and a real estate sales office. The lighthouse, a steel affair, now stands rusting and unused in the woodlands - alone.

About 60 years ago two white families moved to the Island to pursue the shrimping business: the Toomers and the Hudsons.

They were the first ripples of the next population movement to the Island, part of the ebb and flow of life on Hilton Head, matched somehow to a deeper natural rhythm as irrevocable as the tides. The Toomers still own and operate the docks at Hickory Bluff near the spot where Jenkins Island joins Hilton Head. The Hudsons operated the docks on Skull Creek and subsequent to the bridge opening in 1956 began a seafood restaurant right on the docks. This was one of the Island's first restaurants, certainly its first seafood establishment. A few years ago Bennie Hudson sold his shrimping and restaurant business to a young entrepreneur who has in turn made Hudson's Seafood House a nationally known restaurant.

Resting just off Highway 278 beyond the Fairfield Square shopping area is Honey Horn Plantation. Honey Horn is just the thread needed to tie the past of Hilton Head Island to the now and perhaps even the future. Of all the plantations on the Island it is the only one left still functioning to some extent with the same agricultural intent of its ancestors. In 1790 it began as Hanahan Plantation, a name which was altered by time and by Gullah to Honey Horn. The Stoney family purchased Honey Horn in the early 19th century, selling eventually to a William Graham. The Grahams owned Honey Horn in 1863 and lost it to a series of unscrupulous carpetbaggers with names like Dodd, Rivas, Alverez, and so on. During the early 1900's a man named W.P. Clyde bought some 9000 acres on Hilton Head including all that was and is Honey Horn. Mr. Clyde took up residency at Honey Horn. He sold eventually to several northern sportsmen who in turn sold in 1949 to Frederick C. Hack. This tale is significant for two reasons: the Hacks are partly reponsible for the modern era of Hilton Head development, and the progression of Honey Horn points up the pattern of land movement on the Island from the Civil War period to now. In 1872 the Redemption Act was passed to assist land owners in the south to reclaim their lands. It can be said fairly it was a good plan that didn't work very well. Wages needed to be paid to former slaves, rents had to be satisfied, cotton would no longer be king. Some of the lands had

been settled by freed slaves. The Island population of blacks in 1880 was at 3000 and dropped to some 310 by 1920. The various rights to land was, by virtue of sale, squatters' or freedmens' rights, and leases are to this day unclear on some parcels of land. Suffice it to say that by the end of the Second World War the sun was beginning to rise on an Island that showed promise to many men, for a number of reasons.

In 1950 Fred C. Hack, C.C. Stebbins, and Lt. Gen. Joseph B. Fraser purchased 8000 acres of virgin pine forest land on the Island from the Thorne and Loomis families. These three men organized the Hilton Head

Company set up for the purpose of cutting select pine, leaving the hardwoods alone. In 1950 Hack, Stebbins and O.R. McIntosh acquired an additional 12,000 acres for the same purpose. Six portable sawmills were set up, three at each end of the Island. The tall pine was cut and trimmed into boards on the site. The boards were then pulled on carts to a loading dock near what is now Palmetto Bay Marina. This lumber was then barged up the inland waterway to northern cities, or taken down to Savannah where it was either moved inland or loaded onto ships bound for foreign ports.

While they were cutting this timber

they were also looking at the possibility of mining the Island for titanium and rutile and other "rare earths" found to be present in the beach sands in significant amounts. It is a matter of great fortune for the Island that these men had the wisdom and the conscience to elect not to mine the rare earths here. It would have had to be a strip mining operation which would surely have destoyed the beauty and rare natural balance of Hilton Head. They saw, rather, the real value of the Island was its potential for development. The year 1956 truly marks the beginning of the modern Island we now enjoy and experience. In that year the Hilton Head Company's holdings were divided, with General Fraser purchasing half of the company's original holdings on the south end of the Island and the remainder going to the Hacks' and Stebbins' interest. This same year also saw the construction and opening of the first bridge to the Island. It was actually two bridges spanning Mackay Creek to Pinckney Island and then jumping over Skull Creek with a swing span to Hilton Head. It was named the James F. Byrnes Bridge in honor of the former Governor of South Carolina, Secretary of State and Supreme Court Justice. Prior to the bridge, people traveled to the Island by ferry service operated between Buckingham Landing dock (just to your right as you leave the mainland) and a dock on Jenkins Island (now gone). The boat was named "Pocahontas" and operated on a regular basis for 3 years. The opening of the bridge had a major impact on development. Suddenly building materials, equipment, and people were able to come and go freely - Hilton Head lost its isolation and a new era had begun.

In 1957 Charles E. Fraser, a recent Yale Law School graduate, with his older brother Joe, who had been working on the timbering project while Charles was at law school, purchased the family holdings plus an additional 1200 acres and initiated the planning and development of Sea Pines Plantation. Meanwhile the Hack-McIntosh group restructured their holdings almost concurrently beginning work on Spanish Wells Plantation and some speculative homes in Folly Field, and shortly thereafter beginning Port Royal Plantation. This can be perhaps the most confusing part of the Island's history - that is, the development of the modern plantations. The concept was and is basic and simple. These few men began with the idea that large holdings of land could be sub-divided into lots and sold for residential purposes. There was a twist to

64

this. Hilton Head is ideally suited by climate and location for resort activity so the communities developed would have to accommodate both resort and residential activities. It is Charles Fraser who is largely credited with first developing the concept that a resort/ residential community could be successful, if a few special considerations were made. He embodied two excellent and highly compatible interests: the understanding of development and a love of nature and of the natural beauty of the Island. He was at base a conservationist. As a result the concept that has by gentlemen's agreement governed Hilton Head's

development over the last twenty-five years followed these basic precepts:

1) Do not impose development on the environment, blend it in. This is done by using strict architectural covenants governing all building and development in the community. 2) Create adequate green spaces (parks) for the required sense of privacy. And keep density as low as profitably possible. 3) Create roadways for beauty and efficiency, not just fast transit. 4) Build no structure taller than the tallest tree. 5) Cut only those trees that are absolutely necessary. 6) Think always of preserving and enhancing the quality of life for those who

would be residents on the Island. These basic concepts or something close to them were at the heart of Sea Pines Plantation and subsequently in each of the other major developments. Now who and what are they?

Sea pines began master planning and construction shortly after Spanish Wells began a major push to develop. To Charles Fraser, the key was to first build a golf course. This would allow people to come to the plantation for an activity and it would release land for development. Sea Pines grew rapidly, built a second golf course and began construction of Harbour Town, a complete harbour village with shops, restaurants and residential units. Sea Pines built the first condominiums in the state of South Carolina, the Lighthouse Villas. Port Royal, a Hilton Head Company development, was next, just behind Spanish Wells. Subsequent to that the Hacks were bought out of most of the Hilton Head Company by Oxford First Corporation of Philadelphia owned by a man named Aaron Gold. A number of years later, in 1981, Oxford First sold the company to Marathon Oil and shortly after that Marathon Oil was purchased by United States Steel. At this time the Hilton Head Company continues to be the largest land holder on the Island with Port Royal, Shipyard, Wexford and large and assorted commercial holdings. What was once known as Leamington Plantation eventually became the North Carolina Hunt Club and this land after being sold to Phipps Land Company became Palmetto Dunes. Palmetto Dunes was developed like the others with golf courses first and includes an unusual system of ponds and lagoons connnected throughout the plantation and navigable with a small boat or canoe. The former Fish Haul, Seabrook, Myrtle Bank and Pineland Plantations became what is now called Hilton Head Plantation begun by the Sea Pines Company.

So, starting from the north end of the Island, Spanish Wells, Hilton Head Plan-tation, Port Royal, Palmetto Dunes, Shipyard and Sea Pines Plantation are generally thought of as the largest of the plantations. Now added to these are a few smaller but equally lovely newcomers. Opposite Shipyard Plantation on Highway 278 is the Hilton Head Company's new marina-oriented private community called Wexford and next to Wexford is Long Cove, another smaller private golf-oriented community. In the center of the Island across from the entrance to Palmetto Dunes is Shelter Cove, a combination commercial and residential marina village. To the north just before the bridge, on the left you will encounter Windmill Harbour, another private water-oriented residential village. The basic premise upon which the development of the 50's and the 60's rested has to a great extent held on through the last twenty-seven years. Keeping density low and designing structures to blend in as much as possible with the landscape rather than clash with it have remained as priorities.

If golf was the first recreational effort made on the Island, it has, if nothing else, proved successful. There are some 16 championship courses now on the Island with 9 open for resort play. Over the years a number of top amateur tournaments have been played here: the Southern Seniors, Women's Amateur, U.S. Open Qualifying rounds, Super Bowl of Golf, H.H. Celebrity Tournament, and dozens of others. No other community can boast two major professional events as can Hilton Head. The PGA Seniors Tournament held at the Shipyard Golf Club and, of course, the Heritage Classic played on the Harbour Town Links in Sea Pines Plantation are key events on the Island sports calendar. The tradition for the Heritage has been brought from the South Carolina Golf Club of Charlestown, founded in 1786 and reputed to be the oldest such membership golf club in America, thus the name "Heritage" has been applied to the tournament. The headquarters are now at

Island Rugby

the Harbour Town Club in Sea Pines. The Heritage began just on the heels of the Pete Dye/Jack Nicklaus course completion and clubhouse construction in 1969 and has been televised by CBS since the second year. I don't play much golf - just enough to understand what it takes to do it right and to fuel my fascination of the Heritage. The colorful Scottish bagpipe opening parade - the opening cannon blast - the general festivity and glamour surrounding the whole affair are part of the fabric of Island life. It has become the social event on Hilton Head each spring and promises to continue as such. The list of winners is a who's who of golf - Jack Nicklaus, Arnold Palmer, Hale Irwin, Johnny Miller, Tom Watson, are just a few. At the end of the day the players mingle with the crowds and the practice tee galleries are three deep with awe-struck spectators.

The 18th hole of Harbour Town holds a fixed place as one of the nation's great golf holes - with or without the gallery with the lighthouse at Harbour Town towering red and white behind the green and the peaceful sound bordering the massive length of it creating an awesome water hazard. And at the end of the tournament is the awarding of the blazer in the stunning red and green Heritage "Tartan" plaid.

If the Heritage is the star of the golfing year on the Island (there are no months when you cannot play), then the other courses are the icing on the cake. The architects of Hilton Head courses read like a who's who in golf. At Palmetto Dunes, Tom Fazio and Robert Trent Jones; at Hilton Head Plantation, Gary Player & Associates; at the Sea Pines members club, Arnold Palmer was involved. They are all there - in some cases in triplicate. It has been said there are more golf pros per-capita on Hilton Head than in any community in the United States. I know that it's not ture - but there are a fair number. They will videotape your swing and measure the speed of your ball, fit you in some new pants and a shirt and get you

in under 90 before you know what hit you. Former touring pro Bert Yancey makes his home here and operates his world-famous Classical School of Golf in Sea Pines. The Island provides a magnificent setting for these many courses. The deep wooded corridors and ideal growing conditions for grass have conspired to make Hilton Head one of the top golf resorts in the world.

The first golf course, the Ocean Course at Sea Pines, although still a favorite of many, many players, contrasts sharply with the current technology and design of Island courses. Designed in part to be a fine golf course and in part to be a promotional draw for golfers, it proved a difficult task for inexperienced hands. Once the fairways were laid out they had to be cleared; this was largely done by a local man familiar with heavy equipment. He had previously been captain of the ferry boat, put out of work by the Byrnes Bridge. There is no record of how many times he got stuck or how much earth had to be moved or what real rigors were involved in that first project but, rest assured, the task was huge - and the men that set to it were equal to it. The land they began with was mostly low and

flat and that helped. Once cleared and prepared for planting it was hand sprigged by black women who were adept at hand planting. It was not uncommon to see a row of handsome women slowly walking up a cleared fairway pushing springs of grass in as they went, amazingly with their bundles of lunch sitting on top of their heads. Some even carried a melon or a jug of water. It was not uncommon in the early 50's and even 60's to see the native Islanders walking alongside roads with a giant load of laundry or kindling wood, balanced gracefully on their heads. The first pro shop was just a lean-to with palmetto fronds tied together for a roof. It had an oyster shell floor, which Wally Palmer, the Island's first golf pro, says ate a pair of golf shoes every three weeks.

There is a story frequently told by Island golfers (probably apocryphal, at least I know I've never checked it out) about one of the early rounds on that course. Caddies were drawn from willing ranks of Island black men. They had a healthy curiosity about the purpose of these long narrow fairways but little first-hand knowledge of the game of golf at that time. The story goes that a well-known touring pro was encour-

Traditional opening ceremonies of Heritage Golf Classic

74

aged to come and try the course. A few other local dignitaries made up the foursome. As they left the tee and headed down the fairway for the second shot the professional's caddy dropped his golf bag and taking a 7 iron began to run hell-bent-for-leather down the fairway before them. The other caddies quickly followed suit. The player, completely astounded, cried out for them to come back -what was wrong? The last to desert looked over his shoulder and with a smile as wide as Calibogue Sound shouted, "We be back, we be back, jus' got to run down the biggest possum we ever did see!" Having finally accomplished the task the caddies all returned to the astonished foursome - 7 iron, possum and smiles all intact. It was a round of golf not soon forgotten. It wasn't unusual in those days to see all manner of wildlife on the golf course. More than one group had to skip a hole or two to avoid interferring with a family of wild pigs - not a group to be tampered with. Deer, raccoon, possum, and alligators were not unusual sights. Once I saw a pair of wildcats cross a green on the Ocean Course in mid-afternoon - just taking their time - seemingly out on an afternoon stroll. Alligators can still be seen with great frequency in the ponds and creeks that act as water hazards on the Island courses.

Now things are somewhat less wild and woolly. Courses are built and designed on this Island for play and to release land for lot sales. Fairways are measured by laser

beam and cleared and sculpted by men trained to manuever an earth mover like a fine artist. You'll seldom see deer in the daytime on the courses now - but they are still here, in number. The wild cats and boars are gone, but the old alligator is still around - always watching - silent - still - probably wondering what those long legged yellow, pink and green and even purple colored birds are doing smashing a marsh-mallow around on the grass with a stick. Alligators love marshmallows.

Hilton Head had two tennis courts and about 20 enthusiastic players in 1965 - now it has over 200 courts with all manner of surfaces (except grass), many lighted for night play. With Rod Laver at Palmetto Dunes, Evonne Goolagong at Shipyard and Stan Smith at Sea Pines, there is just the slimmest chance you can get instructions. There are year 'round schedules of exhibitions, clinics and tournaments. Hilton Head tennis is highlighted by the Family Circle Cup which has been played on center court at the Harbour Town Racquet Club since 1972, attracting the top names in women's

tennis from the outset. Martina Navratilova, Chris Evert-Lloyd, Billie Jean King, Tracy Austin and Andrea Jaeger are just a few who have played in past events. Within recent years Hilton Head has hosted more televised tennis than any other location. The World Invitational Tennis Classic, the NBC Family Circle Cup, the CBS Classic and the Sea Pines Tournament of Champions have all been sent to the world over TV from the Island. Although it didn't catch on as a popular sport here, paddle tennis was attempted and the first televised platform tournament championship was held here in 1973. For some reason it never achieved the following here at Hilton Head the way it has in New England. Probably because of the warm weather on the Island. Paddle is really a cool weather sport.

Hilton Head lends itself to outdoor sports, however, and if paddle tennis didn't work, others have. Living on Hilton Head is an outdoor experience. The list of activities for the outdoor enthusiast visitor and resident alike is endless. Take, for instance, fishing. There is pond fishing for spot-tail fans and weak fish and bream. There is shore fishing for stripers and bass and even shark. Trolling for bluefish and Spanish mackerel and kings and even an occasional tarpon in the sounds and near offshore waters. Fishing from a boat or off the bridge on the Inland Waterway can produce a South Carolina game fish extraordinare - the cobia. The fellow can exert the force of a fish ten times it size and they aren't small to start with. Some cobia battles go on for hours. And for the big boys there is the "Stream." Sixty miles out and you are into marlin and sailfish and barracuda in the gulf stream. For the last several years Hilton Head has hosted the Billfish Tournament, an event like no other. All the "gold platers," the big boats, Hatteras, Egg Harbour, Bertram, Graves (made right here on Hilton Head) are all in. Each evening they come boiling into harbor with both engines full and the bow throwing a thirty foot spray and on some there is that tell-tale marlin flag. The tournament still holds the state record for blue marlin at 480 pounds. Even the drugstores carry fishing equipment. The tradition goes way back.

There are records of the Elliotts of Myrtle Bank Plantation hooking into giant manta rays (they called them devil fish) and getting a "Calibogue sleigh ride" behind them. For some fishing is fun and a source of relaxation; for others it's the way to survive. Any spring or summer or fall morning you can see the shrimpers head out at 3 am for a day of trolling. These are long hard days of letting the nets down deep and dragging and pulling the nets up and sorting a hundred kinds of fish on a slippery, rolling deck - and doing it all over again until nightfall. Sometimes it's out two or three nights until the catch is in. It's not work that makes a man rich - but it's a life on the sea and Islanders are often men of the sea. The oystermen have to work on the low tide, whenever it comes -in the cool months, just

Island welcome for Wimbledon Champions Evonne Goolagong Cawley and Stan Smith

months with an "R" in them. It is back-breaking labor to fill a bateau with fresh picked oysters and it's not much easier hauling crab traps each day - but it is life "on de riber" and there is no riverman who would ever think of giving it up. If it isn't golf or tennis or fishing, then there is still bicycling, jogging, beach combing, surfing, swimming (there is always the beach - not to mention over 80 swimming pools, both indoor and out - with ocean temperatures ranging in the mid-70's to 80's from May through October), racquet ball, horseback riding, gardening, sailing, canoeing, bird-watching. There are nature parks and trails in both Sea Pines and Hilton Head Plantation. There are opportunities to see white-tail deer, raccoon, possum, alligators (in the warm months) and any of the over 250 species of birds that still visit the Island each year.

Of the Island residents there are two basic persuasions. Those who have come to the Island to retire and those who have not. Retirees come from places like Connecticut, New York, Ohio, Pennsylvania and Washington, DC; they tend to be fairly affluent. Workers come from all over or they were here to start with. Taken together they are characteristically resourceful, goal oriented people, usually intensely interested in every aspect of Island life. Some want to burn

Eighteenth hole of Fazio Golf Course in Palmetto Dunes

the bridge (now no longer the swing bridge but a fixed span four-lane bridge named for Wilton Graves, the State Representative who helped get the concept approved); some want to put two more lanes on to bring in more visitors (there were 750,000 last year). With the major sporting events taking place each year, the Island has become a repository of trained tournament volunteers and tennis officials. The Heritage requires hundreds of volunteers each year, taking care of scoring, communication, marshaling, transportation, even lodging. There are over 120 civic clubs and organizations from Rotary to the Great Books Club to the Barbershop Quartet Group. All members of the community pitch in strongly. This is a place to get involved. There are now some 11,000 residents with a growth rate of 10% per year. These people are lawyers, bankers, insurance salesmen, artists, architects, builders, advertising executives, investment counselors; they are doctors and nurses and ministers and fishermen and restaurateurs; they round out a community that has grown from 4,000 plus 5,000 visitors in 1960 to 11,000 and 750,000 visitors in just 23 years. In the early days (1956 and '57) there were no places for visitors to stay. The Sea Crest Motel was built at the end of Pope Avenue and then Sea Pines built the William Hilton Inn named for the sea captain of the same name. Next came the Adventure Inn named for his ship. Eventually it was considered that the unoccupied homes or the plantations be extensions of the Inn and thus Sea Pines and Port Royal, and later Shipyard and Palmetto Dunes became large extended hotels, and small rental agencies began to pop up to handle all the rental work. Then the Hyatt at Palmetto Dunes was completed, Hilton Head's first major affiliated hotel. Now the Island has the Marriott in Shipyard Plantation, the Holiday Inn, the new Mariner's Inn at Palmetto Dunes, and a greatly expanded Hilton Head Inn (no longer the William

Sixth hole of the Oyster Reef Golf Course in Hilton Head Plantation

Hilton Inn.)

Hudson's, that initial Island restaurant, has been joined by over 100 restaurants and bistros and the Island offers entertainment for everyone. There is a full service hospital with 50 beds and 24-hour emergency room, two medical centers, a private and a public school system from pre-school through twelfth grade, a public library, an AM and an FM radio station, a cablevision station, 2 newspapers, weekly activities and TV publications, six major banks, churches of nearly every denomination, 15 shopping areas - the list is amazing. Somehow I keep reminding myself that this is just a small town - a small, new town.

I recall on that first trip to the Island then 6 years into modern development I was

continually surprised by the place. Everyone seemed to know everyone else. Age was no barrier to friendship. Islanders all seemed to live at the same level - they drew together forming immediate friendships and bonds, much like travelers on a cruise ship do. My first dinner out was in a home with no furniture. We were guests of Sea Pines. Charles Fraser was in the habit of inviting a group of residents over to try the specialties of his new chef. The chef had arrived before the kitchen at the Inn was ready to operate, so Charles simply had him come to the newest house the company had and work on his rack of lamb in the kitchen. Guests used plates brought in for the occassion and sat on boxes and crates and had a feast fit for kings - this happened many times. The Joseph Murtaghs of Painted Bunting in Sea Pines had an annual Halloween party. Everyone on the Island came - at least the newer residents. It was held in front of their home on the beach; there were oysters and hams, and roaring bon fire all blue and red from the salt in the drift wood, and home-made biscuits and everything anyone could think of to drink. The party was the social highlight of the year - everyone wore costumes, nearly every resident of Sea Pines and Port Royal came, some 40 couples. This tradition went on for several years, finally ending when it got too big to handle (no two people could handle an "Island" party after 1974; there were just too many people).

Most of the residents bought supplies in McKibben's Market located about where Ocean One is now on South Forest Beach Road. My mother didn't like it much because there was always beach sand blowing in on the fresh vegetables and meat. The drug counter was located right over the fish and shrimp bins and she said the aspirin always smelled like shrimp. Not long thererafter the Red & White was built at its present location, and for some years was the only supermarket - now there are five. The Red

The Hilton Head Inn

& White became a meeting place - it was where everyone saw everyone else and shopping could take hours. Sometimes at tournament times you'd see Billie Jean King or Johnny Miller buying a cartload of Stouffers' frozen dinners - but you always saw friends. Highway 278 had two lanes, and there were no stoplights on the Island. You could leave Sea Pines and travel all the way to Savannah and not ever stop for a light. You would stop for horsecarts, deer, wild pigs crossing at Fairfield, loose cows and sometimes a game of baseball on the road, but never for stoplights. The post office was at Fairfield Square and it was a twice a week trip. Everyone had a set of large coolers. They were used on the weekly trip to Savannah. This was the way most of the newer residents shopped. Each week a run to Savannah had to be made for the many supplies that just weren't available on the Island. The coolers would be loaded with meat and poultry from Smith's, drugs and sundries from Don Auld's, hardware, clothing, housewares - all were found in Savannah and brought back at the end of the day. Any trip to the doctor was a ride to Savannah as was a movie or concert of any kind.

The regular trips to Savannah were always made early in the morning and it invariably proved impossible to do all the things one had set out to do. To the newest Islanders, Savannah proved to be a strong mixture of both pain and pleasure. Stores seemed not to keep regular hours. Some opened on Wednesday mornings and others on Friday, some opened only afternoons after 2 but, perversly, none of the shops seemed to agree on the hours of business thus two trips a week became the rule rather than the exception. Still, the quiet streets, (traffic was not really too bad in Savannah in those days), the charming gift shops and the quaint little restaurants all conspired to make Savannah a delightful break from Island living. Some basic problems were inescapable. Dry cleaning, for example had to be taken to Savannah - and picked up. Islanders got in the habit of using the same dry cleaner and trips would be switched back and forth. Seldom was a ride to the "city" accomplished for purely selfish reasons. Typically you'd pick up clothing for the Smiths and the Randalls and get a specially trimmed cut of lamb for the Conroys and a few yards of this material or that from the fabric store for someone else. It was a rariety if you didn't see several Islanders in, what was at that time, Gottlieb's Delicatessen-Restaurant on Bull street for lunch. Haircuts and evening meals were often taken at the Downtowner Motor Inn. It wasn't unusual for people to plan a full day in Savannah, spend the night and return the next afternoon after two full days shopping.

The Savannah merchants seemed glad to serve Hilton Head customers, perhaps a response to the reputation Hilton Head was developing for affluent residents. It was difficult to get through a shopping outing in Savannah without at least one, if not more, short discussions about passed opportunities for buying real estate on the Island.

"Oh yes! Hilton Head. I'm going to tell you," the shop keeper would say, "that boy from Hinesville — ahhh Charles Fraser? He tried to sell me some little old chunk of beach-front land. I think he said he'd take $5,000 cash for it. Well, Charlie, I said to him. Charlie, I said, you think my Daddy had a fool for a boy? Well, hell no! Noboby is going to pay $5,000 for a piece of that sand bar you are trying to grow a golf course on. Good luck to ya though. Well, now I look back and only five years down the road this boy has got himself a gold mine. I mean, I could have had half the beach front stuff in Sea Pines for a song. But not me. I figured on what I knew then not what I know now!"

While many of the stories may have been only partly true, there is little question that the maturation process has greatly en-

hanced the value of land on Hilton Head. Early in the planning phases of Sea Pines Plantation lots on the ocean front were marketed for approximately $10,000 to $12,000 apiece. By 1970 the same pieces of land could not be had for less than $60,000. Now, for the very few undeveloped private lots remaining in Sea Pines, a price in excess of $500,000 would not be unusual. Outside of the various Plantations the prices have not been quite as high, but have con-

tinued to rise as the Island has developed.

If there has been a lesson to learn concerning modern life on Hilton Head Island it is, the Island has become a place unsuited for people who are not accustomed to change. The rebirth of the Island with the building of the bridge brought it into the bloodstream of a growing and changing South. The early residents came for many reasons, but the most often repeated were, the climate, the natural beauty of the place

and the relative peaceful, undiscovered atmosphere the Island imparted. Through the years, after a few false starts, the Island took off as a community and in the process became "discovered." Streets have widened, stop lights have been added and the residential areas have grown and developed in response to the demand for Island housing.

For the first years of my parents life on Hilton Head, I was fortunate to be able to visit at least once a year. Even with that amount of frequency, the altered state of the Island continued to surprise me after each visit.

"Well," Pop would say, "The Bank of Beaufort is open every day now." "Remember that dove field we hunted last year? Now it's in the middle of a new community, Sea Pines has started it. They have called it Hilton Head Plantation." It would be foolish to say that all of this rapid growth is pleasing to everyone. There are those who found the Island, and would just as soon roll the bridge up behind them and stop all progress that might encroach on the community they discovered. This reluctance to welcome the absorption of the Island into the mainstream of the Southern growth pattern is a healthy force on Hilton Head and one that has done much to keep the character of this Island community special and apart from so many of the burgeoning towns in the south. It is only by gentleman's agreement and substantial community pressure (however subtle) that the signage on the roadsides has been successfully kept to an acceptable standard, and made it impossible to find any monster 30 story condominium complexes growing out of the dune structure on the sand beaches. The very basis of the structure of the Island is really a feature of the deep and abiding interest and concern of the residents, people who have come from all walks of life and from all corners of the globe.

All reactions to Hilton Head are not the same, this is quite natural. I have an

aunt who comes from a patrician Philadelphia and New York background. She is a lady of great energy and intelligence and not reluctant to voice an opinion. She lives now in a charming house not far from New York City that was built in the early days of the republic. Her first glance and subsequent reaction to the Island residential areas she saw has always stuck with me.

"This," she said, "is a very curious place - looks rather like a bunch of crates in the woods doesn't it?" I suppose it does to someone who has always lived in suburban neighborhoods where home owners were free to a great extent to paint their homes

in any manner they see fit. While there is a sameness to the residential areas on the Island, a closer observation reveals a considerable architectural diversity and choice. The concept of the architectural review board has held fast here. Each Plantation has a board comprised of residents and professional architects established to control the residential construction as much as possible, to protect the existing homes and to safeguard the overall master plan for the community. Any home built in any of the Plantations must pass the test of the review board. Trees are surveyed and specimen trees (especially large or rare) are protected at all costs and size and exterior colors of homes are considered before approval is given. Generally, limiting the pallette of colors to earth-tone stains, stucco or tabby has been the rule. While this particular direction may change from one community to another, the advantage of the review process is apparent. The limiting factors have forced the Island designers to be more creative in developing designs, that make maximum use of space and light and materials. Typically, Island houses seem to attempt to bring the outside in and to create light, spacious interiors in contrast to the natural blending of the exteriors. As the communities have grown, it is interesting to see how nicely the natural treatments of wood and stucco have blended and successfully helped to avoid the appearance of overcrowding.

With all of the dramatic growth and increase in value of Island land it is easy to imagine that much of this has been a dynamic process. Indeed, the legends of land deals, and missed opportunities and struggles to achieve community projects continues in the best of the mainland American traditions. The airport is a good case in point.

You might imagine the changes on the Island have taken place amid much sound and fury. The present airport with its 3,700 ft. paved runway and two terminals is actually the Island's third airport. The first, built about 1957 was in Port Royal near the location of the club house and cart barn. It moved a few years later to a spot transecting what is now the Barony Golf Course; this was a lighted grass strip. Charles Fraser expresssed a desire for the Island to have a larger airport and Fred Hack agreed. But they couldn't agree on a site, so eventually Fraser began clearing a strip for an airport in an area behind the present Lawton Villas. Mr. Hack, realizing all the traffic would then go to the south end of the Island, compromised and provided the present land from the vast Hilton Head Company holdings for the present county airport.

A second generation has grown up on the Island now. Children born to parents who arrived in the 60's are now graduating from college, returning, marrying and beginning the cycle again. As might be expected, the Island has produced a generation of youngsters with an understanding of the sea, a love of nature, in many cases a backhand that will pull the bottoms off your Keds, not to mention an extraordinary crop of fine amateur golfers with four or five touring pro possibilities.

The Island has become the site for a community high school and the elementary school system has been recognized as outstanding in the state. Children grow up fishing; golfing; playing tennis, rugby, soccer, football; swimming, dancing (ballet or tap classes are available), doing gymnastics or working in any of the fine arts.

Early in the development of the Island a few of the better American artists visted here. They liked it and, over the years, others have followed. Men who were at the top of their particular discipline have settled here. Each year the Heritage winner has had a portrait done by Coby Whitmore, a resident and world-famous artist; his friend Joe Bowler has had his paintings hung all over the world. Over the years men like these have attracted other artists; the Island is developing something of a tradition of art. There are now over 6 galleries exhibiting paintings and sculpture.

Perhaps one of the best barometers of any community is the local paper. The Island Packet, published twice a week with its charming Packet boat logo and poetic or literate verse introducing each issue, tells the reader a lot before even a casual study of it. The content is even more telling. Regular features by Island writers talk about history, books, art, film, sports, golf scores, all reflecting the images of a sophisticated readership, ready to devour any number of subjects. People from all walks of life have come here, but the calibre of Island resident is high; yet it is much more than just a community of "our kind of people." Virtually unknown to the rest of the world in 1957, Hilton Head is now known world around as one of the finest South Atlantic coast resorts and residences in the country. Six marinas which handle up to 100 foot yachts have grown from the rickety piers at Palmetto Bay where, not so many years before, fresh cut pine boards were loaded on the barges. Raccoons still get into garbage cans, deer still nibble up the pittosporum, squirrels still steal all the bird feed, the seasons still change as they always have. Of course, the Island is not without its problems. Though issues are looming ever larger - adequate water supply and water treatment facilities, local controls and how they can be made to suit all people of the community - but these are problems faced by communities all over the world, and Hilton Head will face them and prevail.

Life on Hilton Head continues as a reaffirmation of the Island's capacity to delight, surprise and provide. The story of Hilton Head is a story of discovery, first by the wild unknown savages of unrecorded time and then by the Europeans searching for gold and glory - and searching, too, for the limits of their world. Discovery by English planters, the Gullah blacks, the Union Troops, the little school teacher from Connecticut, by the Hacks and the Frasers and the McIntoshs, by my parents, and by me and by you. It is a symphony of sounds all disparate, yet somehow playing together and making up the images of this magical place.

Life on Hilton Head is good, as good as it can be any place on earth because of the Island - yes, and the people - unquestionably, the people. This place, like all others is a part of a continuum. Bill Cornelia's images are frozen moments from that constant electric line of life that is this place. This book is not meant as a definitive history, or a judgement, but rather a composite image of the progress of the Island of Hilton Head in the "Golden Chain" in the midst of the most glorious process of life - the process of becoming.